One-of-a-Kind ⚭ *Wedding*

FAUX FLORALS
and CANDLES

LAURA MAFFEO and
COLLEEN MULLANEY

Creative Publishing
international

Creative Publishing
international

First published in the United States of America by Creative Publishing international, Inc., a member of

Quayside Publishing Group
400 First Avenue North
Suite 300
Minneapolis, MN 55401
1-800-328-3895
www.creativepub.com

ISBN-13: 978-1-58923-392-8
ISBN-10: 1-58923-392-1

10 9 8 7 6 5 4 3 2 1

Library of Congress Cataloging-in-Publication Data

Maffeo, Laura.
  One-of-a-kind wedding. Faux florals and candles / Laura Maffeo, Colleen Mullaney.
    p. cm. -- (One-of-a-kind wedding)
  ISBN 978-1-58923-392-8
  1. Wedding decorations. 2. Silk flower arrangement. 3. Candles. I. Mullaney, Colleen, 1966- II. Title. III. Series.

  SB449.5.W4M34 2008
  745.92'6--dc22

                           2008022233

Cover and Book Design: Sandra Salamony
Page Layout: Sandra Salamony
Photographs: Jack Deutsch Photography
Copy Editor: Carol Polakowski
Proofreader: Julia Maranan

Printed in Singapore

Flowers of all sorts, exchanged by couples as tokens of love, have a deep resonance in our romantic lives. So, naturally, their beauty, form, color, and meaning play a central part in wedding ceremonies and celebrations. From the bridal bouquet to the reception room décor, flowers help make the most of the special day.

Today's brides can choose from a wide array of faux flower varieties and designs. Some may prefer a traditional bouquet of white roses. Others might choose bright magenta dahlias wrapped in ivy or a mix of springtime pastels wrapped in decorative trim.

Candles, in a variety of shapes, sizes, and colors, are another wedding essential. You can showcase candles in many creative ways—from the lighting of the marriage candle to the twilight illumination of a garden path to the design of an elegant centerpiece.

Here are some ideas for matching your wedding flowers and candles with your unique style and personality. Consider the time of day, the time of year, the location, and your theme, too. Your thoughtful choices will transform your wedding into a truly one-of-a kind event.

CONTENTS

Welcome

Benvenuto

WARM WELCOMES

Friends and relatives travel from near and far to be a part of your special day. Why not plan a fun event to extend a warm welcome? Have a barbecue, a cocktail party on the beach, a girls' luncheon, or a thank-you brunch. Welcome gatherings are all about having fun, so keep them light and breezy. Everyone will appreciate the casual feeling and the chance to relax before the big event. Choose a theme or add a game, activity, or another sort of fun-filled twist, but remember: Keep it simple and low-key. The big party is still to come!

BRIDAL TEACUP ARRANGEMENT

Here's a sweet and special, one-of-a-kind favor that your shower or wedding guests will treasure for years to come. This flower-filled teacup is a unique memento to thank friends and relatives for sharing your day. If you want a uniform look and style, buy as many of the same cups as you have guests. Or, for a little variety, hunt through thrift shops and home stores and gather together an assortment of decorative patterns and styles. Either way, these clever giveaways are charming!

Here are the materials you will need to make one bridal teacup:

- one teacup and matching saucer
- one block of floral foam
- three stems of white carnations
- two stems of white spray roses
- three stems of white apple blossoms
- floral snips

STEP 1.   Cut the floral foam to fit inside the teacup, leaving about ½" (1.3 cm) of foam extending above the rim. Be sure the surface is level. Push down firmly to ensure a snug fit.

STEP 2.   Snip the carnation stems to a 2" (5 cm) length.

STEP 3.   Insert the stems around the side of the teacup and toward the center so that the blossoms cover some of the side. Push down at an angle to ensure the stems are firmly in the foam. Space the carnations evenly around the circumference of the teacup to fill in.

STEP 4.   Snip the spray roses to a 5" (12.5 cm) length. Place the roses into the foam in a circular arrangement around the teacup. Make sure the roses are slightly higher than the carnation petals, creating a mound. Fill in all the way around. For more texture, add some buds.

STEP 5.   To make the final layer, cut the apple blossoms to a 6" (15 cm) length. Fill the center with apple blossoms. Be sure the heads are just above the roses to complete the dome shape. If the stems aren't rigid enough, wrap them with a length of floral wire before inserting them in the foam.

Try this!

To make a permanent arrangement, affix the saucer to the cup with ceramic adhesive before you begin. Let the adhesive dry and then make the floral arrangement.

BLOOMING TIER

This flirty arrangement is a tower of texture and color. No matter what the season, it sings of spring. This elegant and dramatic arrangement is perfect for a bridal shower, a welcome reception, or a brunch. The clustered layers of blossoms, arranged in concentric circles, create the old-fashioned look and style of a Victorian nosegay. Select any type of small-blossomed flower in the shades you like best. Apple blossoms, sweet peas, and grape hyacinths are all lovely choices.

Here are the materials you will need to make one blooming tier:

- two 6" (15 cm) terra-cotta pots
- one block of floral foam
- three terra-cotta saucers, one in each size: 4" (10 cm), 6" (15 cm), and 8" (20.5 cm)
- three bunches of mini irises
- three bunches of mini daffodils
- two bunches of tulips
- six to eight leaves from tulip bunches
- hot-glue gun and glue sticks
- floral snips
- floral wire

STEP 1. Turn one pot upside down and center it on the largest saucer. Hot-glue the pot in place. Next, hot-glue the medium-size saucer on top of the base of the glued pot. Hot-glue the smallest saucer on top of that, upside down. Finally, glue the second pot onto the upside-down saucer. Let the terra-cotta tiers dry thoroughly.

STEP 2. Cut the floral foam into small rectangular blocks. Glue the blocks onto the lip of the bottom pot.

STEP 3. Continue gluing foam onto the second tier. Cut foam to shape to fill the top pot. Trim all the corners that stick out past the edges.

STEP 4. Cut iris stems to 2" (5 cm) in length and hot-glue them into the foam. Arrange the flowers around the base, keeping the heads even. If a stem sticks out too far, simply cut the stem and try again.

STEP 5. Just as you did for the iris, cut the daffodil stems to 2" (5 cm) in length and glue them around the second tier. Be sure the tier is filled in with blossoms to create a full and rounded look.

STEP 6. Arrange the tulips in the top pot, trimming the stems as needed to get the height and shape you like. Start positioning the flowers at the center of the pot, making those stems the longest. Work out to the sides, trimming the stems to length so the flowers form a slight dome shape.

STEP 7. After you've added all the tulips, fold each leaf in half, base to tip, to create a loop. Wrap the ends of the leaf together with floral wire. Push the wire securely into the foam in the top pot. Arrange folded leaves around the entire outside of the pot to add a final layer of color, texture, and interest to the tier.

More Ideas

BEACHSIDE HURRICANES

A sunset wedding is magical—especially when the sun is setting over the ocean. Here's a natural decorative detail that can create an over-the-top romantic effect. Pour a small amount of sand into tall glass candleholders of any shape. Position a white or neutral-colored pillar candle securely in the sand. Next, add a random selection of pretty shells, colorful bits of sea glass, and other ocean treasures, such as starfish or small pieces of driftwood (you can find all of these in craft and floral supply stores). Scatter more shells and sea glass around the candleholder to complete the tablescape.

ALL-AMERICAN WELCOME BOUQUET

This simple red, white, and blue bouquet in a basket makes a patriotic statement—and is a fun addition to a summer event that falls around Flag Day (June 14), the Fourth of July, or another date that has personal meaning for you. The blue-and-white bandana adds color and a touch of country whimsy. This basket of blooms is a perfect arrangement for an outdoor luncheon, brunch, or barbecue. Of course, you can simply change the colors of the carnations and bandana to create a theme and color scheme of your own.

SWEET REHEARSAL DINNER CENTERPIECE

Rehearsal dinner décor and centerpieces should be casual and fun. Save the formal touches for your wedding day. This ring of flowers is made of bright orange and red ranunculus, deep purple hyacinths, and simple greenery. Glass cylinders of staggering heights are filled with assorted, colorful candies. The center cylinder contains a floating candle.

FRUIT TERRARIUM

Make your guests feel right at home with these simple, colorful terrariums. Clear glass containers with matching lids come in assorted shapes and sizes. They're perfect for housing fresh-looking faux lemons and Granny Smith apples such as these—or any other type of fruit in colors you prefer, depending on your season or theme. You can also fill the containers with colorful candies or glistening holiday ornaments. Add a color-coordinated welcome card—perhaps even in the native or ancestral language of your family or guests—printed on heavy cardstock to personalize your greeting.

GERBERA DAISY BLOCK

These bright and cheery gerbera daisy blocks add a dramatic splash of color. These hot-orange shades are great for a sunny afternoon event. Choose a pale pastel for a bridal shower or white flowers for a glamorous evening affair. Simply secure the blooms to foam cubes with hot glue. Cubes come in several sizes. You could also stack them or arrange them side by side to create a brilliant tablescape.

PATHWAY, AISLE, AND ENTRYWAY DÉCOR

What better way to make a dramatic entrance than with colorful flower arrangements and glowing candles? Add a bit of romantic elegance to a walkway by placing a series of floating candles to guide your guests' footsteps. If the path is in a natural or wooded setting, sprinkle handfuls of rose petals, too, to mark the way. Frame a stairway with dramatic iron candelabras for a grand, illuminated entrance. For the ceremony, hang small buckets brimming with seasonal foliage at the ends of the pews to decorate the aisle with simple, elegant style.

DOORWAY DROP FESTOON

Small details can make a big impact. These flower balls are a simple but glamorous welcome to the ceremony—whether hung from an exterior iron railing, as shown here, or suspended next to doorways or on interior beams or arches. Smaller versions make an ideal decoration at the edges or corners of a chuppah, the canopy included in traditional Jewish wedding ceremonies. As you plan, consider the style of the architecture in your location, the best and most visible positions for hanging, and any floral or decorating restrictions.

Here are the materials you will need to make one doorway drop festoon:

- one 12" (30.5 cm) plastic-foam ball
- two large bunches of flowers (one each of cranberry and purple)
- 2 yd. (1.8 m) of $\frac{1}{2}$" (1.3 cm)-wide ivory satin ribbon
- floral pin
- one roll of 2" (5 cm)-wide white satin ribbon
- floral snips
- hot-glue gun
- floral wire
- scissors

STEP 1.   Cut all the blossoms off the flowers so that the stems are short, about 1" (2.5 cm), as shown here. Press one blossom stem into the plastic-foam ball and push down to hold it in place. Glue around the stem to secure it. Repeat with the remaining blossoms until the entire ball is covered.

STEP 2.   Loop the narrow ribbon around the flower ball four times, leaving a 16" (40.5 cm) length of ribbon for a tail at each end. Push the floral pin around the center of the loops and secure the ribbon to the ball.

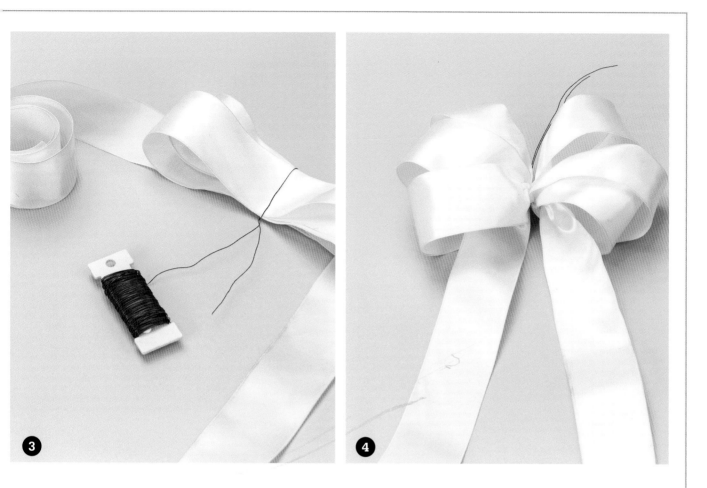

STEP 3.   To make the bow, fold the wide ribbon to make four loops, leaving a length of ribbon approximately 18" (45.5 cm) in length for a tail. Roll out the ribbon another 18" (45.5 cm) for the tail at the other end. Holding the center tightly, wrap floral wire around the ribbon and twist a few times to secure.

STEP 4.   Squeeze the wire together to make the bow bunched and full. Fluff out the loops. Cut the wire. Trim the ribbon ends straight across or at an angle, whichever you prefer.

FLORAL ARCH

Floral arches are a lovely way to embellish an entryway, whether it's the entrance to the ceremony, the reception, or any other event. By simply weaving together an array of your favorite flowers, you can create a fantastic frame for the occasion—and a gorgeous backdrop for photos! This arch has a base of green ivy, which makes it easy to fasten bunches of blue hydrangeas, ribbon-tied wheat, hops, and lilies securely. Make small arrangements with the same flowers for chair swags, napkin décor, or even the bride and groom's car.

Here are the materials you will need to make one arch:

- three 6' (1.8 m) lengths of ivy
- two large bunches of wheat (16 to 20 stems each)
- natural-colored raffia
- eight blue hydrangeas
- sixteen white lilies
- five stems of hops
- 3 yd. (2.7 m) of 1$\frac{1}{2}$" (4 cm)-wide sheer ribbon
- floral wire
- floral snips

STEP 1. Lay the three lengths of ivy side by side. Beginning at one end, firmly wire the strands together to form a strong, lusciously full base for the other elements.

STEP 2. Break the wheat to make small lengths. Form small bunches of six or seven stems each. Tie each bunch with a short length of raffia.

STEP 3. Cut the stems of the hydrangeas, lilies, and hops to about 3" (7.5 cm) in length. Starting at one end of the ivy base, wrap in the flowers and sheer-ribbon bows with wire, creating an attractive sequence as you go. (The sequence shown in the photo on page 24 is hydrangeas, lilies, and hops, followed by a bow with two bunches of wheat.)

STEP 4.   Continue working in sequence until you have filled in the entire length of the floral arch.

Try this!

To make a full bow, form three loops with the sheer ribbon. Wire the base of the loops, leaving a length of ribbon for the tail. Cut the wire and wrap in place.

More Ideas

SWEETHEART WREATH

Love is truly in the air with this peony-covered heart, hanging in the window at the reception, on the church's front door, over the bride's and groom's seats at the dinner table, or even above the wedding cake display. Fashioned from a heart-shaped grapevine base adorned with ivy tendrils and blousy peonies, this wreath is accented with a few white lilies. Of course, all the blossoms are faux, so you can make it well ahead of the wedding day. Instead of peonies, you could also choose roses, magnolias, or another big-blossomed flower.

PAPER BAG LUMINARIAS

Candlelight instantly adds romance to any setting, especially on a warm summer evening. These simple paper bags are an ideal way to illuminate a pathway for your wedding guests. Look for colorful bags that match your décor or theme. For an easy, artistic touch, punch shapes in the top edges with a decorative hole punch—available in star, heart, or many other shapes. You'll also need a glass votive and candle for each bag. The votive will protect the flame and provide a weight for the bag.

FLORAL PEW BUCKETS

These autumnal adornments set the stage for your ceremony and decorate the wedding aisle with high style. Orange lanterns, berries, and assorted foliage make a seasonal accent for the crimson peonies and chocolate cosmos. All the stems are secured in foam. Tie small tin buckets to the pew ends with a length of cream-colored satin ribbon. When the ceremony is over, you can untie the buckets and display them at the reception.

FLOATING CANDLE PATHWAY

Gently lead your guests to the ceremony, the cocktail area, or dinner reception with these floating candles and a blanket of pretty flower petals. Each glass hurricane contains a brightly-colored blossom in its base and a single floating candle. To add a little more light, place another one or two floating candles in each hurricane. To sweeten the air, float scented candles. The petals scattered in the pathway add romance and drama—and even help mark the way, especially after night falls.

ENTRYWAY CANDELABRAS

These candelabras light the way with understated elegance that won't break your budget. You can find these simple iron frames—or others like them—at any large craft store. Wrap the frames in lengths of ivy, stephanotis, and deep-purple lisianthus blossoms. Mount the frames with white pillar candles and tall, glass candleholders that not only add to the design but also protect the flames from drafts and breezes. For more illumination, position votive candles along the steps, making sure to keep them to the side, out of the flow of traffic.

SPECIALTY FLOWERS

Specialty flowers are those little extra details that set your wedding apart. After you've selected the flowers for your bridal bouquet, you still have lots of other flower choices to make: the bouquets for the bridesmaids and maid of honor; the flower girl's basket and barrettes; boutonnieres for the groom, groomsmen, and father of the bride; and corsages for mothers and grandmothers. All the flowers you choose should reflect the style, theme, and colors of your wedding—and coordinate with the clothing, of course—to ensure that you and your party are high on aisle style.

TWO FLOWER GIRL BARRETTES

Being a flower girl is a very big deal to a little person. The responsibility can be quite exciting and maybe even a little overwhelming. Let the little girls in your life know how much you appreciate their taking part in your special day. These sweet and simple barrettes—in two styles—are a great gift that will do just that. Your flower girl will love them long after she has proudly skipped down the aisle.

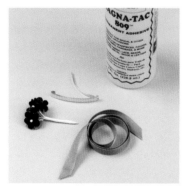

Here are the materials you will need to make one of the bunched flower barrettes:

- one small bunch of velvet appliqué flowers, about 2" (5 cm) long
- one metal barrette, about 1³/₄" (4.5 cm) long and ¹/₄" (6 mm) wide
- fabric craft glue
- approximately 6" (15 cm) of ³/₈" (1 cm)-wide grosgrain ribbon
- small paper clip

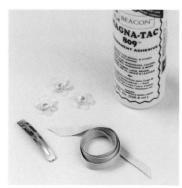

Here are the materials you will need to make one of the appliqué flower barrettes:

- approximately 2" (5 cm) of ³/₈" (1 cm)-wide grosgrain ribbon
- one metal barrette, about 2" (5 cm) long and ¹/₄" (6 mm) wide
- fabric craft glue
- three small fabric appliqué flowers, about ³/₄" (2 cm) wide (choose flowers that will sit flat)

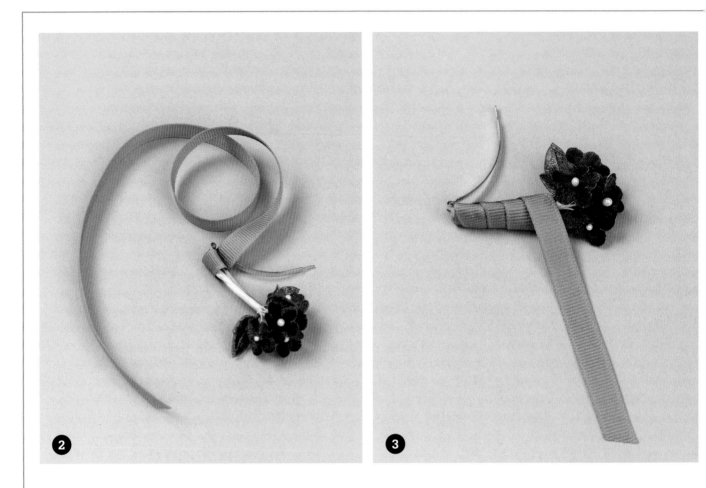

To make the bunched flower barrette:

STEP 1.   Glue the stem of the flower bunch to the top of the barrette so that the flowers are sticking out of the top. Let the glue dry completely.

STEP 2.   Secure one end of the ribbon to the bottom inside of the barrette with a small amount of glue. Let the glue dry completely.

STEP 3.   Wrap the rest of the ribbon tightly around the barrette until the entire stem is covered up to the base of the flowers. Secure the ribbon end to the inside of the barrette with a small amount of glue. Hold the ribbon in place with a small paper clip until the glue dries.

STEP 4.   Trim any ribbon that sticks out beyond the barrette.

To make the appliqué flower barrette:

STEP 1. Cut a piece of ribbon the exact length of the barrette and glue it to the top. Let the glue dry completely.

STEP 2. Glue the three flowers onto the barrette so that they are evenly spaced and the two on each end overhang the barrette end slightly. Allow the glue to dry completely.

FLOWER GIRL BASKET

As dainty as the little one carrying it, a flower girl basket should have a personality all its own. This basket is feather-light, and the handle gives little hands something to hold on to in case of stage fright!

For a winter wedding, cover the basket with deep-red anemone blossoms and wrap the handle with red velvet ribbon. For autumn, choose chrysanthemums in a rainbow of colors, paired with a bit of foliage or berries. Orchid blossoms are ideal for a tropical summer look.

Here are the materials you will need to make one flower girl basket:

- five hydrangea heads in soft green and pink tones
- one small, unfinished basket
- 1 yd. (1 m) of decorative ribbon
- hot-glue gun and glue sticks
- scissors

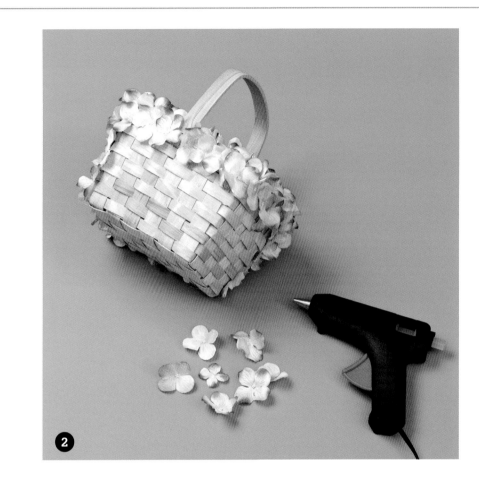

STEP 1. Remove all the blossoms from the hydrangeas. Cut off any traces of the plastic stems at the base of the blossoms.

STEP 2. Working with the glue gun, glue individual blossoms to the sides of the basket. Layer the blossoms so the surface of the basket is completely covered. Let the glue set.

STEP 3. Place one end of ribbon flat along the inside of one end of the handle. Hot-glue the ribbon end in place.

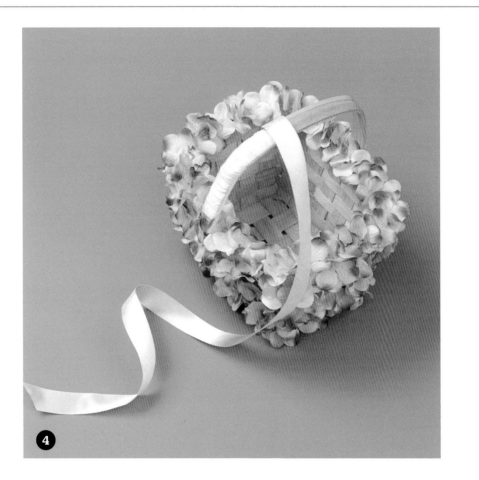

STEP 4.   Wrap the ribbon around the handle, holding it taut as you go. Layer the ribbon wraps so that just the ends overlap, to create a smooth surface on the wrapped handle. Continue wrapping until the entire handle is covered.

STEP 5.   Cut the ribbon from the spool and glue the end in place at the base of the handle.

Try this!

Choose a type of flower that has a flat bottom so it adheres securely to the surface of the basket.

VICTORIAN NOSEGAY

Traditionally, each flower in a Victorian nosegay had a special meaning. Roses meant love. Lilies meant devotion. A nosegay is made of rings of several types of flowers, which creates a stunning circular design. Just as it was during the late nineteenth century, today the nosegay is a truly romantic arrangement, perfect for wedding celebrations. Make nosegays for yourself and your bridesmaids. You might want to make a petite version for your flower girl, too. These sweet bouquets are charming and easy to carry.

Here are the materials you will need to make one Victorian nosegay:

- one stem of purple ranunculus
- five stems of paper whites
- twelve stems of grape hyacinths
- eight stems of lavender sweet peas
- 34" (86.5 cm) length of 2" (5 cm)-wide decorative ribbon
- floral wire
- floral snips

STEP 1.   Discard all of the flower foliage so that you are left with only stems and blossoms. Hold the stem of ranunculus and gradually add stems of paper whites to surround the central flower. Keep turning the bunch to form a neat circle.

STEP 2.   After you have added all the paper whites, wrap wire around all the stems, just under the flower heads, so that the blossoms hide the wire.

STEP 3.   Next, add the grape hyacinths, placing them slightly lower than the paper whites to create a lovely dome shape. Make sure you place the hyacinths at the same height all around to define the shape of the circle.

STEP 4.   Wrap the hyacinths with wire as you did the paper whites.

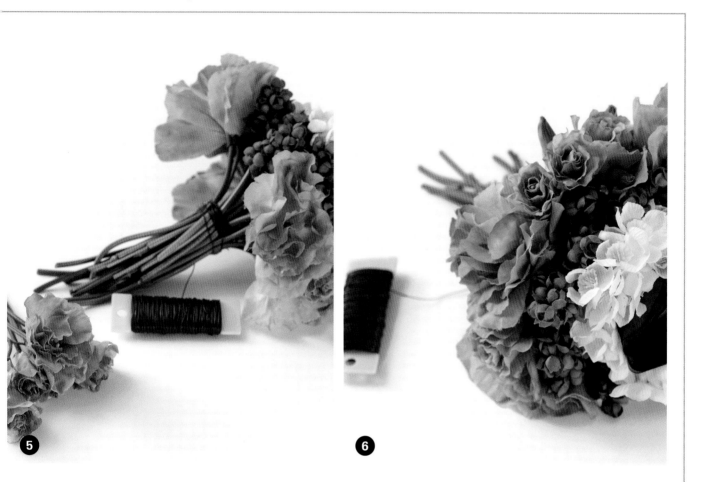

STEP 5. Now add the sweet peas. Again, be sure to turn the arrangement so you distribute the flowers evenly. The sweet peas should be slightly lower than the hyacinths to keep the dome shape uniform.

STEP 6. Wrap all the flowers with wire, cut the wire, and secure the end.

STEP 7. To add the ribbon, make large loops and attach them to the trunk with wire, arranging the loops evenly.

More Ideas

BRIDE'S HAIRPIECE

Swept-up hairstyles are elegant and
fashionable and quite popular among
brides these days. This simple floral
accent couldn't be easier to make.
Choose a large blossom to match or
complement the flowers in your bouquet.
Attach a wide plastic comb to secure the
flower to your hair. Sew or glue on a short
veil of netting to finish the look perfectly.
Netting is available in different patterns
and colors, too. Comfortable to wear and
lovely to look at, you'll want to keep this
understated hairpiece on all day long.

BRIDESMAID'S
FLORAL HEADBAND

This sweet and simple headband is so
easy to make, you can quickly fashion
one for every member of your bridal
party. Simply wrap a purchased cloth or
plastic hair band with a length of light-
blue ribbon (or a ribbon in the color of
your choice). To attach the single flower
blossoms (in a color that matches the
ribbon), simply glue them to the top
of the band, leaving the ends partially
free of blossoms so the band will lie flat
against the wearer's head. Glue more
blossoms to a flower girl basket, ballet
slippers, or other accessories to create a
complete look.

MODERN BOUTONNIERE

The boutonniere is a flower arrangement, worn on a man's lapel. The bride and groom present these flowers to the groomsmen, fathers, grandfathers, and other important men in the couple's lives. Most often, the boutonniere is made of a single flower featured in the bride's bouquet and the rest of the wedding flowers. This sleek, modern version—a crisp, white orchid blossom wired together with simple greens—is sophisticated and stylish. Orchids, a popular modern flower, are becoming more prevalent in brides' bouquets and wedding décor.

VINTAGE CORSAGE

Part of the wedding tradition is to present flowers to the mothers, grandmothers, godmothers, and special aunts of the bride and groom. Often, the flowers take the form of corsages. The colors and flowers are selected to complement the wearer's outfit. Corsages can be worn on the wrist or pinned onto a dress or handbag. These cream-colored antique garden roses, surrounded by soft waves of velvet ribbon, give this corsage an understated elegance—a perfect combination for a wedding with old-world charm.

TABLE ACCENTS

What would a wedding celebration be without plenty of great food and beverages to entice and entertain your guests? As part of your festivities, be sure to decorate your dining tables and serving stations to set the mood. It's easy to add an extra-special touch with colorful faux floral garlands and topiaries. Candles and candle pots are perfect accessories, too. Pay particular attention to self-serve dessert buffets, champagne bars, and other places where you know your guests will linger.

SAND ART ARRANGEMENT

If you'd like a bit of modern flair, this simple arrangement is just what you're looking for. The black and white layers of sand are all about fun, and the bright yellow centers of the blossoms add a pop of color. You can buy decorative sand in a variety of colors at craft and floral supply stores. Pick a color combination that complements your wedding theme or décor. For a summer affair, add a few small seashells to the sand. If nighttime glamour is more your style, add sparkling sequins and colored gems.

Here are the materials you will need to make one sand art arrangement:

- small round glass that fits into square glass container
- block of floral foam
- 10" (25.5 cm)-wide square glass container
- two bags of craft sand (one black, one white)
- ten stems of white alliums
- scissors
- floral snips

STEP 1. Cut the floral foam to fit into the small round glass. Push down firmly on the foam so the top is level with the top of the glass.

STEP 2. Place the glass into the center of the square vase. Pour some of the black sand into the square vase, turning the square vase slowly as you pour to distribute the sand evenly.

STEP 3. Tap the square glass lightly to settle the sand and even the surface so it's level.

STEP 4. Pour in a small amount of white sand to create the next layer. Keep turning the square vase to make sure the sand is even and level.

STEP 5. Continue to pour alternating levels of black and white sand, turning as you pour, until you reach the top lip of the square vase. After pouring each layer, tap the glass lightly to even the surface.

STEP 6. Cut the allium stems to 6" (15 cm) in length.

STEP 7. Insert the allium stems into the floral foam in the round glass. Arrange them so that they conceal the space between the center glass and the square vase.

STEP 8. Bend the stems slightly to overlap the top edges of the vase. Be careful when transporting this arrangement so the layers of sand won't shift.

SUNFLOWER TOPIARY

Wine bars are an increasingly popular feature of modern wedding celebrations—and a far less expensive option than full bar service. Draw your guests close and treat the eye with this tall and elegant tabletop accessory. This autumnal arrangement is made with vibrant sunflowers that set a sunny mood. The natural moss and wood elements have an organic, woodland appeal. As an alternative, choose large blooms that match your own wedding season or décor. Select complementary colors and accessories to complete the tablescape.

Here are the materials you will need to make one sunflower topiary:

- one block of floral foam
- one 8" (20.5 cm) terra-cotta pot
- one bunch of mixed sunflowers, with twelve to fourteen blooms
- one 6" (15 cm) plastic-foam ball
- one stem of mixed fall leaves
- 8" (20.5 cm) square of moss
- small grouping of grapevines
- cluster of autumn berries
- scissors
- floral snips
- floral pins
- hot-glue gun and glue sticks

STEP 1. Cut the floral foam block to fit inside the terra-cotta pot. Hot-glue the foam in place to secure it.

STEP 2. Cut all of the leaves, blooms, and flower stems off the main stem of the sunflower bunch. You'll be left with a rugged-looking "trunk." Push the stem into the center of the foam block and hot-glue it to secure.

STEP 3. Snip all of the flower stems to 3" (7.5 cm) in length.

STEP 4. Press one sunflower blossom into the plastic-foam ball and hot-glue it to secure. Continue positioning the sunflower blooms until the ball is covered.

STEP 5. Cut the stems of the leaves so they are very short, as shown. Gently fold the leaves in half lengthwise and glue the stem and leaf bottom in between the sunflower blooms. Continue adding leaves to give the ball a full and colorful autumnal look.

STEP 6.   Find a free space in the center of the plastic-foam ball. Push that section of the ball onto the stem in the pot.

STEP 7.   Arrange the moss on top of the foam block in the pot. Cut or tear away any extra moss hanging over the edge.

STEP 8.   Gather the grapevines and trim the ends with floral snips. Insert one set of ends into the floral foam block, close to the base of the stem. Press the ends firmly and fix in place with a floral pin. Twist the vines around to the back of the sunflower ball and adhere to the ball with a floral pin.

STEP 9.   For the finishing touch, you'll need one sunflower blossom, a few leaves, and the autumn berries. Glue the leaves and berries to the moss first. Then glue the sunflower blossom on top of the leaves. Let the glue dry thoroughly.

More Ideas

DAHLIA VOTIVE

Simply set in beautiful faux dahlia blossoms, these small votive candles make bright, cheery accents for any wedding celebration. These pretty arrangements provide the perfect way to dress up cocktail tables, line a walkway, or—when arranged in a luxurious cluster—add a bold accent to the center of the table. Dahlias are a showy flower, available in a wide variety of colors, so choose any shade that suits your season, theme, or décor. Add a gently scented candle for a bit of extra interest. Try making flowery votives with large garden roses, peonies, football chrysanthemums—even small cabbages.

SWEET CANDLE POT

This soft and frilly candle pot is perfect for the tablescape of a bar or buffet table. The soft pink shades of the faux sweet peas accent the dramatic black and white of the classic toile-pattern tablecloth. Simply line a decorative urn with floral foam. Insert several stems of sweet peas—cut to the desired length—so the blooms are distributed evenly around the outer rim. Bend the stems and tendrils to create a natural, cascading look. Place the candle in a plastic candleholder and affix it to the floral foam. Firmly place the glass hurricane over the candle.

BLOOMING CANDELABRA

Together, gold and white are the essence of elegance. This S-shaped swirl base (from a home accessories store) is outlined with a length of ivy garland, secured with wire wraps. Assorted all-white faux flowers—gerberas, lilies, and stephanotis—are layered on top of the ivy for a fully in-bloom appearance. Wide white pillar candles continue the moonlight-white theme. A tall arrangement like the one shown here is perfect for tables that need some height, such as a champagne or coffee station. You can make the same stunning arrangement with a different-shaped base and with shorter pillar candles, too.

DELICATE TULLE DRAPE

Give your dessert table the sweet attention it deserves with this petal-filled tulle drape. Measure the table length and width to determine how much tulle you'll need. Add a bit extra for cutting and draping. Fold the tulle in half lengthwise and fill the fabric with faux blossoms or petals. Tie the fabric at the ends and center with decorative ribbon to create the gentle draping. Tack the ends and center to the table edge. You'll find tulle in a variety of colors and widths at most craft stores. This special touch is also perfect for gift, guestbook, or champagne-toast tables.

REGAL GARLAND ROPING

It's so easy to add those little extra touches that make all the difference. Showcase your bar table with a simple frame of garland blooms (maybe even come up with a special signature drink for your guests). These brightly colored yellow and orange marigold blossoms are simply glued onto lengths of wide satin ribbon. You can buy these inexpensive flowers in bunches. The large, blousy flower heads fill the ribbon quickly. The tablecloth is solid white with a 2 yd. (1.8 m) length of paisley fabric centered on top to create a colorful, textured underlay for the garland and the glassware.

HANGING DÉCOR

Fill the air with bright, twinkling lights and bundles of flowers suspended in space. Hanging décor adds a special ambience to your one-of-a-kind day. Imagine how your guests will feel as they stroll beneath a flower-wrapped chandelier or gather to chat by the light of paper lanterns in a rainbow of pastels. There are many ways to add the whimsy and charm of hanging décor to any type of wedding event—sure to make any wedding event truly special and unique. These simple decorative details are easy to make and are cost effective, too. A little goes a long way.

MONOGRAM WREATH

This initial in bloom is a lovely way to proudly display the bride and groom's new shared monogram (or you can display one initial for each last name). This personalized floral makes beautiful signage for leading guests to the door of the rehearsal dinner or reception. You can hang it on a fence, doorway, or even a tree trunk with a decorative ribbon in the color of your choice. Any flower with small, compact blossoms will work well. Red, white, and rosy flowers add an especially romantic touch.

Here are the materials you will need to make one monogram wreath:

- 16" × 20" (40.5 × 51 cm) piece of poster board
- delphinium blossoms in light and dark rose tones (ten stems' worth)
- large letter template (optional)
- hot-glue gun and glue sticks
- decorative ribbon in color of your choice
- pencil
- scissors

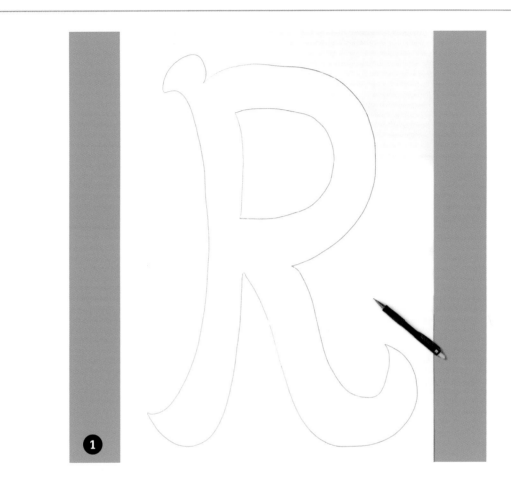

STEP 1.   With the pencil, draw a large, freehand letter of the bride and groom's monogram onto poster board. (If you prefer, you can trace a template of the letter.) Choose a fancy, formal script or a simpler shape, depending on the style of the rest of your wedding décor.

STEP 2.   Cut out the letter with scissors.

STEP 3.   Working with the hot-glue gun, glue the blossoms onto the surface of the letter. Arrange the flowers so the dark and light shades create a pleasing pattern. Be sure to cover the edges of the paper well. Let the glue set completely.

STEP 4.   To display the monogram wreath, loop the ribbon around the top at center. After you've attached the wreath to the perfect spot, tie the ribbon with a big showy bow.

KISSING BALL

Here's a modern twist on the Victorian-era hanging decoration known as the kissing ball. Full of colorful faux blossoms instead of the traditional evergreens, this kissing ball is accented with delicate tendrils of ivy, contrasting flowers, and a lovely wide ribbon. Start with a floral ball, found in most craft stores, and add your personal touches for a quick and easy transformation. Tie the shimmering ribbon in a bow and hang it any place you choose. Change the colors of the blossoms and ribbon to match your theme and décor.

Here are the materials you will need to make one kissing ball:

- one stem each of purple- and magenta-colored blossoms
- one craft ball covered with white roses
- one bunch of variegated ivy
- 1½ yd. (1.4 m) of decorative wire-edged ribbon
- floral snips
- floral pins

STEP 1.   Snip the magenta-colored blossoms to 2" (5 cm) in length. With floral pins, secure the stems to the floral craft ball, pressing them in place firmly. Continue adding magenta blossoms until you have positioned them evenly around the ball.

STEP 2.   Cut the purple blossoms to 2" (5 cm) in length. Again, secure the stems with floral pins, pressing firmly into the ball. Work around the ball, filling in the spaces to create a nice pattern of color.

STEP 3.   Cut the ivy tendrils to 2" (5 cm) lengths. Arrange the ivy evenly around the floral ball, filling in more of the spaces between the blossoms.

STEP 4.   Leaving a tail at one end, fold the ribbon to make four loops. Leave the rest of the ribbon free to form the other tail. Gather the loops at the center with a floral pin. Press the ribbon securely into the center top of the ball. One loop is the hanging hoop. Fluff the others to form a full bow.

Try this!

Most craft stores sell simple wedding accessories in special sections or aisles. Shop for ready-made blooms and ribbons to suit your style and turn simple into sensational!

More Ideas

FLOWER-FILLED CHANDELIER

Hanging décor makes a great impact but requires very little effort and expense. This chandelier has one large and several small glass vases, which are filled with water to add a realistic touch. In each vase, a combination of fuchsia and apple blossoms are artfully arranged. This floral accent is perfect to hang in an entryway or over the dance floor. To make a stationary variation, remove the chain and place the large vase on an iron candle stand. Add a few drops of food coloring to the water for a burst of color or submerge glitter, gems, or glass marbles to add more pizzazz.

LANTERNS AND LIGHTS

Weddings are happy celebrations, so why not add some whimsy and fun to your decorations, too? This combination of colorful paper lanterns, string lights, and paper streamers instantly adds a festive air—and is sure to fit any budget. You'll find a wide variety of choices in mail-order catalogs, at craft stores, and on the Internet. The combination of colors, the number of strands, and the arrangement are all up to you—you can't go wrong. When the sun sets, the bright colors and twinkling lights will keep your party going long into the night!

COLORFUL VOTIVES

Set your wedding softly aglow with these easy-to-make twinkling lights. Simply twist lengths of wire to craft hoop frames for each glass candleholder. Fill each holder with a colored votive candle. Votives come in a variety of colors, from vibrant to pastel, and in several scents, if you'd like. You can choose one color or combine colors to suit your theme and style. These lavender and blue shades evoke an English garden. For a more traditional look, choose all white. Hang the individual votives in clusters anywhere you'd like to add interest— from the garden to the reception hall or on paths in between.

PAPER DOILY CONES

Whimsical details are often the most memorable. Hanging cones filled with small bouquets of flowers have an especially sweet look—whether they are hanging on the front door of the reception room, the end of a pew, or even on the bride-to-be's bedroom door. Roll and glue paper doilies to form the cone. Then fill them with a small mix of flowers of your choice and hang them with decorative ribbons. These delicate cones also make a lovely bouquet for your flower girl, as they are small, lightweight, and very pretty.

SPECIAL DETAILS

Small and special details can make an extra-big impact. Carefully chosen accents and accessories add an element of surprise and delight to your wedding events—a bouquet of delicate posies in the powder room or ballet slippers adorned with sweet blossoms for your ballerina flower girl. What about dressing up your favorite pooch for the occasion with a festive collar of flowers? These decorative touches say a lot about you and your sense of style. They're also light on time required and easy to fashion— but will be sure to attract a lot of attention from family and friends.

ROMANTIC CHAIR SWAG

The soft shades of this vintage-style arrangement create a feeling of romance. Clusters of old-fashioned flowers are accented with sprigs of ivy and a bow flourish. Not only is the decoration beautiful in itself, it's functional, too. Make a swag for each end chair on the aisle to mark off the rows reserved for family and members of the ceremony. Tie long tails of satin ribbon across the aisle before your guests arrive. Then cut the ribbons as members of the family and bridal party enter to take their seats.

Here are the materials you will need to make one romantic chair swag:

- one stem of purple hydrangea
- one stem of lilac garden rose
- one stem of blue delphinium
- one stem of viburnum
- 18" (45.5 cm) length of decorative sheer purple ribbon
- four 12" (30.5 cm) lengths of ivy
- floral wire
- floral snips

STEP 1. Gather the flowers to make a small bouquet. Cut the stems to equal length—about 6" (15 cm). Arrange the flowers so that all of the blooms are visible on one side of the bouquet. Wrap the stems together with wire.

STEP 2. Form a bow by looping the sheer ribbon several times. Wrap the base of the loops with wire to secure them.

STEP 3. Arrange the ivy tendrils in a crisscross pattern to form a star shape. Be sure the ends splay to create interest and to give the arrangement a wide base. Wrap the tendrils together with wire.

STEP 4.   Attach the swag to the chair with a strong, covered wire. If any wire
shows, simply make a small bow to conceal it. Or, you can tie the swag
on with a wide, strong ribbon or a decorative cord. Be sure to choose
a section of the chair that will hold the swag in place securely—for
example, through a rail or slat.

FLOWER GIRL BALLET SLIPPERS

With just a few buds and bows, you can easily turn ballet flats into adorable footwear for your flower girls. These adorable shoes are a one-of-a-kind accessory that will complement the color of the girls' dresses and the flowers in the bouquets they carry, too. Simply choose store-bought shoes in your color of choice, then glue on the small clusters of faux roses and velvet ribbons. You can find faux rosebuds and velvet ribbon in every sweet color you can imagine!

Here are the materials you will need to make one pair of ballet slippers:

- pair of ballet flats
- 1 yd. (1 m) of $3/8$" (1 cm)-wide velvet ribbon
- one stem of roses
- needle and thread
- hot-glue gun and glue sticks

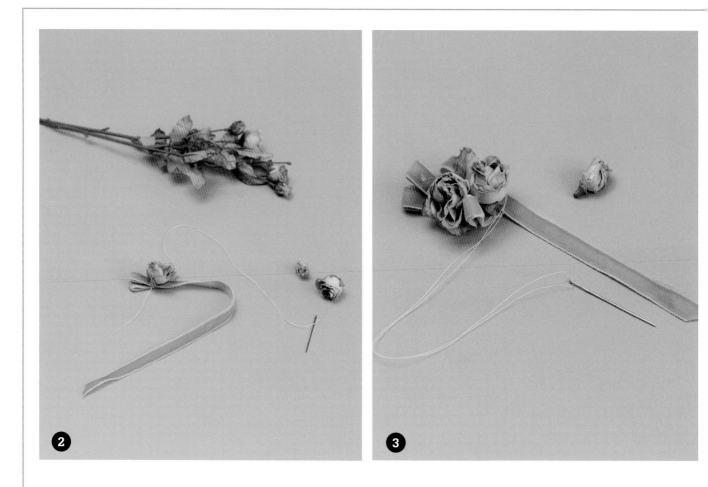

STEP 1. Cut the velvet ribbon in half. Fold one end over twice to form small looped petals.

STEP 2. Remove the rosebuds from the stem. Hand-stitch several onto the ribbon to create a small cluster.

STEP 3. After sewing on the buds, fold the other end of the ribbon to form two more petals.

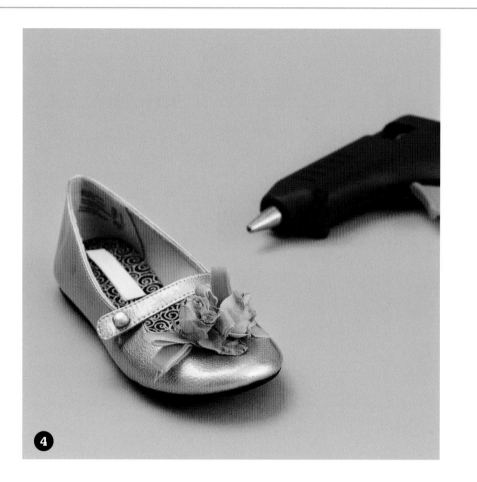

STEP 4.   Hot-glue the rosebud cluster to the top of the ballet slipper, positioning
it at center. Clip the ribbon ends to length if necessary. Set the slipper
aside to allow the glue to dry thoroughly.

STEP 5.   Repeat the steps to make a matching rosebud cluster for the other
ballet slipper.

More Ideas

CALLA LILY FISHBOWLS

Show off your sense of style with this one-of-a-kind decorative detail. The simple, modern lines and exotic blooms add a sophisticated touch to your champagne table or buffet. This dramatic and clever design is made simply by stacking three large fishbowls (very economical!). Each bowl contains three white calla lilies. The flower stems are twisted to fit the shape of the bowl, which adds to the bold graphic design. If the stems are too long or the ends are discolored, snip off the excess. Other types of flowers—tulips, lilies, and cosmos, to name a few—will work well, too.

SPARKLY CAKE TOPPER

One of the highlights of the reception is cutting the cake. Some couples display the cake during the entire reception—to whet appetites—and some simply wheel it out before it's served. Either way, guests look forward to the viewing and, of course, the eating of the cake! This cake topper is fashioned from peach-toned ranunculus blossoms. The stems are cut short and glued to a cardboard cake form. Jeweled strings, shaped and glued in between the blooms, form sparkling loops. Design your topper so it embellishes the cake but doesn't overpower it. Choose colors and flowers that mirror your theme and wedding décor.

POWDER ROOM POSIES

This pretty pairing is an unexpected and eye-catching surprise. You'll impress your guests with your attention to details, too. This vase is filled with spring lilacs, but you can choose any type of faux blossom that suits your style and décor. Purchase a tall plastic container, a short glass candleholder, and a scented or unscented votive candle. Wrap the vase and glass with wire-free ribbons in coordinating colors and patterns, overlapping the edges slightly as you wrap. Glue the ribbons in place. In no time, you'll have an easy and elegant accent that will make your guests feel special in any room.

GUESTBOOK BLOSSOMS

The small, eye-catching touches do make your wedding a one-of-a-kind affair. This petite grouping—the perfect accent for your guestbook table—will do just that. The sophisticated white lilies balance the vibrant lemon-lime ribbon and green berries in a short, simple glass vase. It's sure to make all of your guests stop to sign their names and express good wishes for the bride and groom. The best part about this arrangement is that, after the reception, you can present it as a gift to thank someone who has worked hard to help you prepare for your special day.

BEST FRIEND'S COLLAR

Here's a way to dress up your favorite pooch for the big day. Be sure the collar fits around your pet's neck comfortably—if it's irritating, he'll roll on the ground and crush the flowers. Start with a generous length of ivy vine. Snip the blossoms off stems of faux flowers and wrap each short blossom stem with floral tape, from top to bottom. Attach the blossoms to the ivy securely with wire. Make a hook closure with a short length of wire at each end of the ivy. If your dog is the sensitive type, instead make a small bouquet to secure to his everyday collar with a soft ribbon or cord so he doesn't notice quite as much. Either way, he'll steal the show!

CHAIR BACK FLORAL CLUSTERS

Decorating chair backs is an easy and inexpensive way to make a spot look pretty. Special chair backs can also designate special seating for family members, the bridal party, or the bride and groom. The gem tones in this colorful chair back express a bright, celebratory mood. The small bouquet of roses, lisianthus, viburnum, and ivy is festive and slightly formal. Centered on the chair back, this floral cluster is ideal for the bride's and groom's ceremony chairs, to be admired by guests during the ceremony. After the ceremony, move the couple's chairs to the reception room to accent the head table.

SEASONAL TOUCHES

The four seasons offer a bounty of fresh ideas and creative inspiration for the design of your faux floral and candle accessories. If your wedding is in the spring, you might choose flowers and delicate buds in soft, pastel colors. For a summer affair, have some fun with vibrant citrus orange, lemon, and lime tones in various intensities. Autumn offers the many colors of changing foliage for inspiration. Transform your winter wedding into a wonderland of frosty whites and sparkling gem tones. When planning your events, from the engagement party to the reception, Mother Nature is a great place to start.

BUTTERFLY NAPKIN RINGS AND VOTIVES

Springtime is a lovely time for a wedding. Flowers are starting to bloom, and all of nature is coming back to life after a long winter. Capture the fresh feeling of the season with these butterfly votives and napkin rings. They are easy to make and coordinate beautifully with most floral designs. You'll find everything you need at craft or floral supply shops. When the wedding day is over, let these butterflies fly away with your guests as special keepsakes.

Here are the materials you will need to make one napkin ring and one votive:

- one small glass votive, $2^3/_4$" (7 cm) tall by 2" (5 cm) wide

- one votive candle, in color of choice

- one twig ring, $3^1/_2$" (9 cm) in diameter

- six to eight paper butterflies with wire stems, ranging in size from $1^1/_2$" to $2^1/_2$" (4 to 6.5 cm) wide

- brown paper-wrapped wire, 6" (15 cm) in length

- hot-glue gun and glue sticks

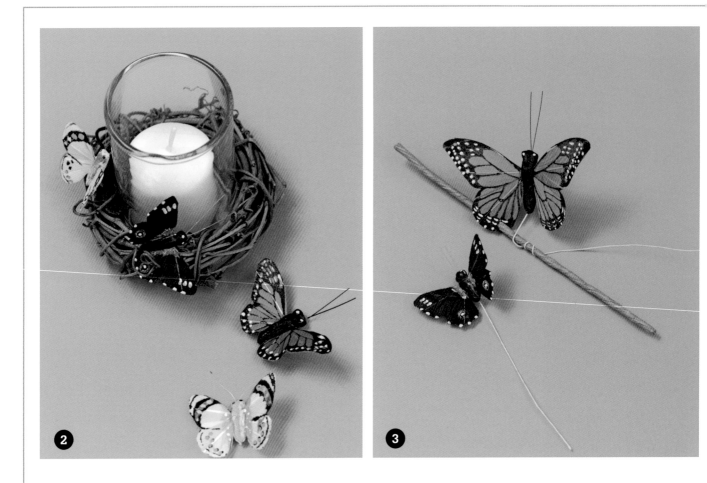

STEP 1.   Place the glass votive inside the twig ring. The ring should fit snugly around the bottom of the votive.

STEP 2.   Remove the stems from four butterflies of assorted colors. Hot-glue the butterflies to the twig ring.

STEP 3.   Next, make the napkin holder. Attach two of the butterflies, one large and one small, to the center of the paper-wrapped wire by wrapping their stems around the wire tightly.

STEP 4.   Bend the paper-wrapped wire to form a tight letter C. If necessary, squeeze the wire a bit tighter after you've wrapped it around the folded napkin for a more secure fit.

Try this!

Bend the paper-wrapped wire around the glass votive to make sure each napkin ring is the same size and shape.

FALL LEAF CYLINDER CANDLES

Autumn is rich with colors and textures. Fortunately for brides planning fall weddings, these natural elements create an instant, dramatic backdrop. Accessorize with seasonal designs of your own. These cylinder candles have the look of a first frost, warmed by the soft colors of falling faux leaves. A light coat of spray paint adds the frosty finish. Set these candles on a welcome table, bar, or buffet table. Line a pathway, brighten the reception hall, or create a tablescape by grouping them with scattered faux berries and leaves.

Here are the materials you will need to make one fall leaf cylinder candle:

• one bunch of faux fall leaves

• iron

• one glass cylinder vase

• 8" (20.5 cm) pillar candle

• ivory or white spray paint

• spray adhesive

STEP 1.   Set the iron to a medium-hot setting. Press the leaves so they're completely flat. If the leaves are still bumpy, wet them slightly and press again with the iron on a high setting. Let the leaves dry thoroughly.

STEP 2.   Turn the leaves so they are underside up. Spray the undersides liberally with the spray adhesive to coat well, following the manufacturer's instructions.

STEP 3.   Press the leaves firmly onto the surface of the cylinder vase. Arrange the leaves around the cylinder to create a pleasing pattern. As you work, hold each leaf in place until it is affixed securely.

STEP 4.   Working in a well-ventilated area, spray the leaf-covered cylinder with a light coating of the spray paint. Lightly coat the leaves, too, for a frosty effect. Let the paint dry thoroughly.

More Ideas

SPRING BRIDAL BOUQUET

When designing your bouquet, choose flowers that complement the style, theme, and season of your wedding, but also set off the style and color of your dress or gown. These classic, romantic pastels are especially well suited for a springtime wedding. Peonies, roses, lisianthus, and lavender delphiniums are woven together in a dome-shaped cluster. Pearls are a wedding tradition, and strings of the faux variety are a great alternative to ribbon, adding texture, sparkle, and elegance. The string-pearl-wrapped stems add to the luscious appeal of this full and frilly bouquet.

SUMMER BRIDAL BOUQUET

Summer is the perfect time of year to be extra colorful and vibrant. These hot-orange lilies are as sun drenched as the season itself. The possibilities for summery, tropical flowers and colors are endless. Working with seasonal florals ensures you'll find plenty of choices in floral supply and craft stores, too. Experiment by mixing in vivid citrus tones of lemon and green. Add some complementary sky-blue shades to increase the intensity. In this exotic bouquet, the colors of the red ranunculus and blue iris are repeated in the bright colors of the patterned ribbons.

SUMMERY CANDLES AND BLOOMS

Cascading flowers and bright, citrus-tone candles make this decorative trough an ideal summer arrangement. It makes a beautiful statement whether you place it indoors or out. The blousy blooms include ranunculus, bells of Ireland, viburnum, orchids, and hydrangeas. Trailing flowers, like these orchids, make a natural-flowing extension at the corners of the rectangular, textured container. Nestled among the flowers are three lime-green pillar candles. The candles are affixed securely to floral foam with plastic candleholders, which are easy to find in most craft stores.

TWO NAPKIN ACCENTS

You can easily fold a cloth napkin to create a pocket, which is the perfect place to insert a dazzling decorative floral. These two fiery blossoms—a full and bold chrysanthemum, perfect for an autumn wedding, and a sweet and delicate nasturtium, perfect for late spring or summer—are just two of the many seasonal florals you can choose from. Morning glories, jasmine, orchids, clematis, and mandevilla vines are all lovely choices. Scatter faux fruits or extra blossoms across the tabletop as an accent. Experiment with color by setting a contrasting-color napkin against a crisp, white linen tablecloth.

AUTUMN BRIDAL BOUQUET

This gorgeous autumnal bouquet is a play on rich shades, textures, shapes, and patterns. Five oversize roses are surrounded by cranberry-colored hydrangea, ranunculus, and feather accents. Gather the stems together and wire the stem tops securely. Pin one end of a wide, colored ribbon to the stem tops with a pearl-headed pin. Wrap the ribbon around the stems, working from top to bottom and overlapping the ribbon slightly as you wrap. Pin the ribbon again at bottom and trim any excess. You'll be holding your bouquet for a while, so comfort is a factor, but you'll carry this lovely ribbon-wrapped bouquet with ease and style.

WINTER BRIDAL BOUQUET

The bouquet is surely the bride's most important accessory. Choosing the flowers is a very personal matter. For example, you may want to showcase your own favorite flower type, the first flower your fiancé gave you, or flowers that you both love. In this striking bouquet, magnolias are set off by a few orchid stems, which add color and texture. The black and white striped ribbon is a bold eye-catcher, especially if the bride is wearing a white dress or gown. For a softer and more formal look, wrap the flower stems in a wide blush-toned satin ribbon instead.